High-Functioning Anxiety for High-Achieving Women

A 30-Day Guide to Calm Overthinking, Strengthen Emotional Boundaries, and Restore Mental Clarity

Disclaimer

By reading or using this guide, you agree to the terms of this disclaimer. If you do not accept these terms, discontinue use.

This guide is for informational and educational purposes only. It is not professional advice of any kind, including but not limited to financial, legal, business, psychological, or career counseling. The author is not a licensed professional in these fields, and reading this guide does not create any client, advisory, or professional relationship.

You should consult qualified professionals regarding any decisions related to your personal, financial, legal, business, or psychological situation. Do not treat the content of this guide as a substitute for professional guidance.

The information provided is based on research and personal interpretation. While efforts were made to ensure accuracy, the author and publisher make no guarantees or warranties regarding completeness, reliability, or suitability of the material. You assume full responsibility for how you choose to use this information. To the fullest extent permitted by law, the author and publisher disclaim all liability for any loss, damage, or consequences arising from your reliance on this guide.

No specific results, achievements, or outcomes are promised or implied. Individual experiences will vary.

Any tools, brand names, concepts, or examples referenced are the property of their respective owners and are used for informational purposes only. Their inclusion does not imply endorsement. Any individuals appearing in cover or promotional images are stock models used under appropriate licenses.

Table of Contents

Introduction

High-functioning anxiety shapes the lives of many high-achieving women, often remaining unseen by others. These women may appear calm, organized, and accomplished, efficiently handling demanding jobs, family duties, and social obligations. Internally, they often grapple with persistent overthinking, worry, and self-criticism. This guide clarifies how high-functioning anxiety affects high-achieving women and explains why managing overthinking, setting emotional boundaries, and maintaining mental clarity are essential.

Although not a clinical diagnosis, high-functioning anxiety represents a recognized pattern. Anxiety and stress can fuel productivity, but often at a personal cost. Many women cope with anxiety by over-preparing, taking on extra responsibilities, and rarely relaxing. They become reliable problem solvers, anticipate others' needs, and strive for excellence, sometimes leading to exhaustion.

The distinction of high-functioning anxiety lies in the gap between outward accomplishments and internal stress. Women may manage deadlines and lead teams successfully while experiencing constant worry, persistent overthinking, and pressure to achieve perfection. Achievements provide only temporary comfort, as new concerns soon arise.

External influences such as societal expectations, workplace pressures, and cultural standards can reinforce this relentless pace. Career-driven women balancing multiple roles may feel compelled to excel without showing vulnerability. This dynamic can cause ongoing tension, reduce the enjoyment of success, disrupt sleep, and strain relationships.

Three main challenges often emerge: chronic overthinking, weak emotional boundaries, and mental fog. Overthinking can extend beyond work, resulting in cycles of second-guessing and rumination that drain energy and make relaxation difficult. Blurred emotional boundaries can lead to overcommitment and taking on others' stress, increasing the risk of burnout and lowering self-worth. As urgent tasks accumulate, mental clarity can fade, making it hard to prioritize and feel satisfied.

Recognizing these challenges marks the beginning of change. This 30-day guide provides a structured approach to move from survival mode to a sense of empowered calm. Each day's practice is brief and adaptable to fit a busy schedule.

In this guide, you will learn:

- Techniques for cultivating calm through daily mindfulness, deep breathing, and sensory awareness (days 1 to 10)

- Methods for setting and maintaining emotional boundaries, communicating needs clearly, and protecting your energy (days 11 to 20)
- Practical tools for restoring mental clarity, including time management, digital detox, and regular self-check-ins (days 21 to 30)

You will also find journaling prompts for self-reflection, morning and evening rituals for intention-setting, and guidance for handling setbacks. This guide does not promise instant results. Instead, it helps you change your relationship with anxiety by focusing on sustainable habits and self-compassion. The goal is to reclaim calm and clarity while pursuing what matters most.

If you find it difficult to make time for yourself or worry that slowing down could impact your achievements, this guide offers practical, realistic steps to help you thrive. Begin your journey toward calm and resilient clarity, one day at a time.

Understanding High-Functioning Anxiety

High-functioning anxiety is both elusive and persistent, especially among women with demanding ambitions and high standards. From the outside, everything can look successful and controlled. The internal experience, however, often tells a far more complex story. This chapter explores the specific traits, symptoms, and pressures at play, providing a clear foundation for understanding the unique shape that high-functioning anxiety takes in high-achieving women. We will also clarify how to distinguish healthy ambition from patterns driven by anxious perfectionism, and why self-awareness forms the bedrock of meaningful change.

Common Traits and Triggers in High-Achieving Women

High-achieving women with high-functioning anxiety tend to share a handful of defining traits. They are often conscientious, ambitious, and organized, holding themselves to exceptionally high standards in everything they do. Colleagues and friends might describe them as reliable, diligent, or even "unflappable." Yet beneath this calm surface, a different set of patterns typically emerges.

Some common traits include:

- An internal drive to achieve more, paired with a persistent sense that even the highest accomplishments might not be "enough."
- Reluctance to delegate, rooted in concerns that others will not meet the same standards or that mistakes will reflect poorly on them.
- Exceptional planning and organizational skills, sometimes bordering on over-preparation or micromanagement.
- A strong focus on anticipating and averting potential problems, which can spiral into chronic worry.
- Difficulty relaxing or "switching off," leading to restlessness even during downtime.

The triggers for high-functioning anxiety often come from the same environments where these women succeed. High-pressure work projects, tight deadlines, competitive teams, and changing family roles can all increase worry and stress. Even positive opportunities, such as a promotion or a leadership role, can trigger anxiety as responsibilities and expectations grow.

In social situations, triggers may include fear of disappointing others, speaking in public, or being more visible than usual. Comparing oneself to others, both in daily life and on professional or social platforms, can deepen self-doubt. For many women, the thought of not meeting external expectations is enough to start a cycle of anxious overthinking.

Symptoms and Daily Manifestations

High-functioning anxiety does not always look like the textbook definition of anxiety. Instead, symptoms are woven into the daily habits and thoughts of those affected. While there may not be obvious panic or avoidance behaviors, the internal tension and overdrive become a way of life.

Some key symptoms include:

- ***Overthinking***: Persistent rumination about potential outcomes, what-ifs, or how decisions might be judged.
- ***Restlessness***: A sense of urgency or agitation, making it hard to slow down or be present with loved ones.
- ***Sleep difficulties***: Racing thoughts at bedtime, trouble falling asleep, or frequent waking in the night.
- ***Perfectionism***: Obsessive attention to detail and discomfort with "good enough" work, often resulting in inability to finish a task.
- ***Procrastination***, paradoxically driven by fear of imperfection or making the wrong choice.
- ***Physical symptoms*** such as headaches, digestive issues, muscle tension, or fatigue, which may go unrecognized as anxiety-related.

- ***A busy schedule packed with work***, commitments, volunteer roles, or social obligations, which leaves little or no time for true rest.
- ***Difficulty asking for help or being vulnerable***, due to fears of appearing incompetent or disappointing others.

These symptoms manifest in moments both big and small. A manager leading a project might obsessively revise emails before sending, fearing minor errors. At home, the same person could struggle to relax with family, mentally replaying workplace conversations instead of being present. Even "relaxation" is approached as another task, to be scheduled and optimized rather than genuinely enjoyed.

Distinguishing Healthy Ambition from Anxiety-Driven Perfectionism

Having goals and expecting a lot from yourself isn't a bad thing. These traits often drive people to succeed in their work and creative pursuits. The tipping point is when healthy motivation slides into anxiety-driven perfectionism.

Healthy ambition is characterized by:

- Setting challenging, realistic goals.
- Working steadily toward improvement.
- Accepting setbacks as opportunities to learn, rather than evidence of inadequacy.

- Experiencing satisfaction and pride in completed work, regardless of whether it is flawless.

Anxiety-driven perfectionism, on the other hand, is marked by:

- Chronic feelings that success is never enough.
- Intense fear of failure or negative evaluation.
- Tendency to catastrophize even minor mistakes.
- Relentless self-criticism, often accompanied by indecision and avoidance.

These differences matter because perfectionism rooted in anxiety often drains energy, narrows perspective, and increases the risk of burnout. It may lead to chronic dissatisfaction, even when real achievements stack up. Over time, this cycle can erode self-confidence and an individual's enjoyment of her own success.

Societal and Workplace Pressures

High-functioning anxiety in women develops within social and professional environments that strongly shape how it appears and persists.

Societal expectations play a major role, especially for women managing multiple responsibilities. Traditional gender roles continue to place pressure on women to succeed at work while also appearing to be ideal caregivers, partners, and friends. Media and social platforms reinforce the message that women should "do it all" and make it look easy, which increases internal pressure and self-criticism.

Workplace pressures often overlap with these cultural expectations. High-achieving women in competitive settings may face:

- Direct or subtle pressure to outperform male colleagues or constantly prove their value
- Bias in evaluations or access to opportunities, leading to the belief that they must exceed every standard to be seen as capable
- Work cultures that reward constant availability and long hours while discouraging flexibility
- Vague or changing expectations that increase overthinking and self-doubt

Even workplaces that support diversity and inclusion can still place hidden demands on women. High-performing women are often expected to manage emotions, resolve conflicts, support others, or take on unpaid and unrecognized tasks. These added responsibilities can make anxiety feel normal and harder to question or address.

Self-Awareness as the Foundation for Positive Change

Recognizing high-functioning anxiety is not about labeling yourself or focusing on flaws. It is a starting point for understanding both the challenges and the strengths common among high-achieving women. Self-awareness shifts anxiety from something hidden and isolating into something visible and manageable.

Building self-awareness involves simple but meaningful practices:

- Noticing thought patterns and behaviors without criticizing yourself
- Identifying personal triggers and how they affect mood, focus, and energy
- Reflecting on where perfectionism or overwork comes from, whether it is driven by personal values or outside pressure
- Paying attention to physical signs of anxiety, such as shallow breathing, tension, or difficulty concentrating

This process does not require quick fixes or major life changes. Instead, it creates space for steady and lasting improvement. When women can clearly recognize anxious patterns and understand how these connect to their strengths, they are more able to make thoughtful choices about workload, boundaries, and self-care that support their long-term goals.

Self-awareness also helps when dealing with outside pressure. By understanding the source of anxiety, women can better decide which responsibilities truly belong to them and which ones can be shared or released. Over time, this clarity strengthens resilience and opens the door to healthier and more sustainable ways of thriving.

In the next chapters, you will find tools and exercises to deepen awareness, reduce anxious overthinking, and build greater calm and focus. You can begin now by simply observing your thoughts, physical sensations, and emotional responses. These small acts of attention form the foundation for everything that follows.

If you are worried about the intensity of your anxiety or how it affects daily life, consider seeking support from a qualified mental health professional while working through this guide. This chapter offers general guidance and is not a replacement for medical or therapeutic care.

The Science Behind Overthinking

Overthinking rarely appears openly. Instead, it weaves into daily routines as a constant stream of analysis, replaying events, and considering what-ifs.

High-achieving women with high-functioning anxiety often recognize overthinking as both familiar and difficult to escape. To break this pattern, understanding how overthinking operates beneath conscious thought is essential. This chapter explains the science behind overthinking: the cognitive loops that maintain it, the stresses that increase it, the inner dialogue that intensifies it, and the ways it disrupts well-being. We will also review evidence-based reasons for interrupting this cycle, preparing the way for effective strategies in later chapters.

Cognitive Patterns That Drive Overthinking

At its core, overthinking results from the brain's cognitive processes working excessively. Human brains naturally analyze problems, anticipate challenges, and look for patterns. These abilities historically improved survival and success. However, when these processes turn inward and go unchecked, they create ongoing overanalysis.

Several cognitive patterns drive overthinking:

- ***Rumination***: Repetitive thinking about past mistakes or unresolved issues. Rather than finding solutions, rumination keeps the mind fixed on the same details, often increasing regret or anxiety.
- ***Catastrophizing***: The mind imagines the worst possible outcomes. For example, an unanswered email might trigger fears of professional failure.
- ***All-or-Nothing Thinking***: Thoughts shift to extremes, such as complete success or total failure, leaving little space for nuance or self-acceptance.
- ***Perfectionism***: The urge to review decisions repeatedly in search of a flawless answer traps the mind in cycles of doubt.

These patterns evolved as mechanisms for caution and improvement. Problems arise when they become habitual, increasing pressure without producing new insights or meaningful action.

The Impact of Chronic Stress on the Mind

Chronic stress, especially prevalent among high-achieving individuals managing numerous responsibilities, exerts a profound impact on brain chemistry and mental habits. When stress persists, the body repeatedly activates the fight-or-flight response, releasing adrenaline and cortisol. These hormones prepare the body for immediate action, but sustained high levels disrupt normal brain function and overall well-being.

Exposure to stress hormones alters neural circuits in brain regions involved in mood regulation, memory, and decision-making. The amygdala becomes more sensitive, leading to heightened emotional responses. The prefrontal cortex, essential for planning and focus, experiences reduced activity and connectivity. As a result, individuals often find it difficult to redirect their attention away from worries. This leads to a rigid focus on perceived threats, even when they are minor or unlikely to occur.

Chronic stress also impairs working memory and the ability to prioritize important information. The mind becomes inclined to detect potential dangers everywhere, reinforcing patterns of overthinking. This state of constant vigilance makes it challenging to break free from cycles of rumination. The brain, conditioned to anticipate negative outcomes, resists efforts to relax or shift perspective.

Understanding how chronic stress affects the mind highlights the importance of effective stress management. By addressing the underlying causes and adopting coping strategies, individuals can restore healthier brain function and reduce the mental burden associated with ongoing stress.

The Role of Self-Criticism and Inner Dialogue

The way a person speaks to themselves has a strong effect on overthinking. Self-critical thoughts are especially common among people who hold high standards and push themselves to achieve.

Negative self-talk often sounds like this:

- "I should have done that better."
- "Why do I keep making mistakes?"
- "Everyone else seems to manage this easily."

These thoughts form a harsh inner narrative that keeps worry and doubt active. When someone criticizes themselves for overthinking, it adds another layer of judgment, which deepens rumination instead of resolving it.

Research in cognitive behavioral psychology shows that frequent self-criticism is linked to higher anxiety, difficulty making decisions, and ongoing stress. It weakens self-trust, making it harder to take healthy risks or tolerate uncertainty. It also limits mental space, leaving little room for creativity, problem-solving, or new perspectives.

Noticing the inner critic without reacting to it is an important first step toward change. Trying to force these thoughts away rarely works. A more helpful approach is to respond with self-compassion and to learn how to tell the difference between inner dialogue that supports growth and inner dialogue that disrupts calm and balance.

How Overthinking Sabotages Focus and Well-Being

Some reflection supports adaptation and growth, but chronic overthinking undermines cognitive performance and emotional health.

One significant effect is reduced focus. When the brain repeatedly revisits the same concerns, directing attention to tasks that require concentration becomes difficult. This mental noise can:

- Slow decision-making because each choice receives excessive scrutiny and doubt.
- Block creativity, as the mind remains occupied with rehearsing past events and regrets instead of generating new ideas.
- Cause procrastination or avoidance, making tasks appear overwhelming due to excessive internal debate.

Overthinking also affects the body. Mental strain often leads to chronic tension, fatigue, and irritability. Many people experience poor sleep, struggling to fall asleep or stay asleep as racing thoughts persist at bedtime.

Emotional well-being also declines. Persistent restlessness or dissatisfaction may develop, as unresolved concerns continually overshadow personal achievements. This pattern reduces satisfaction in daily accomplishments and relationships, drains motivation, and increases the risk of burnout.

Understanding the science behind overthinking can be empowering. Recognizing these patterns is not about blaming yourself. It is about beginning with informed self-awareness. When you notice cognitive habits, observe how stress affects you, and pay attention to your inner dialogue, you create a strong foundation for real change.

The tendency to overthink may not disappear completely. It is often part of being a thoughtful and capable person. With awareness and intention, however, you can learn to interrupt unhelpful cycles, treat yourself with greater kindness, and direct your energy toward what truly matters.

In the next chapters, you will be introduced to practical tools and daily exercises designed to reduce mental noise and restore calm. Step by step, you will gain a clearer understanding of how your mind works and how to guide it toward greater clarity and balance.

Cultivating Calm: The First 10 Days

The initial days of any new journey play a crucial role in shaping long-term success. High-achieving women who experience racing thoughts and restlessness may find the transition from awareness to action particularly challenging amid the fast pace of daily life. This chapter presents a focused ten-day plan to stabilize a busy mind, offering practical tools that encourage calm without becoming overwhelming. Each day's activities build grounding habits that slow mental activity, increase clarity, and prepare you for deeper personal work.

10-Day Plan for Calming Racing Thoughts

Consistency drives change. By practicing targeted exercises for ten consecutive days, you begin to reshape your response to overthinking. This plan offers brief, accessible practices that integrate smoothly into your daily routine. The exercises require no special equipment and minimal additional time, making them practical and sustainable.

The ten-day structure provides a clear progression:

Day 1: Breathing Space

Practice a two-minute deep breathing exercise in the morning and evening. Focus on inhaling slowly through the nose and exhaling through the mouth, noticing the sensation of your breath.

Day 2: Sensory Reset

Take a midday sensory break. For three minutes, concentrate on your surroundings by observing visual details, listening to ambient sounds, or noticing textures you can touch. This anchors attention in the present moment.

Day 3: Body Awareness

Complete a brief body scan at bedtime. Lie comfortably and systematically notice each part of your body, releasing tension as you move from head to toes.

Day 4: Thought Log

Each evening, spend five minutes journaling any recurring or persistent thoughts. Writing them down can help clarify patterns and lessen mental clutter.

Day 5: Morning Clarity

At breakfast, set an intention for your day with a simple ritual. This could include writing a motivational phrase or noting a specific goal, supporting a more focused mindset.

Day 6: Mindful Commuting

During travel, dedicate a few minutes to mindfulness. Pay attention to your posture, your breath, or the movement of your body, fostering calm before daily activities.

Day 7: Evening Check-In

Reflect for three minutes on your day's experiences and emotions. Acknowledge what feels challenging or positive, which can support emotional regulation.

Day 8: Safe Place Visualization

During stressful periods in the afternoon, close your eyes and visualize a calming, safe environment. Engage all your senses to make the scene vivid and comforting.

Day 9: Gratitude Focus

Identify three things that brought comfort or gratitude during the day. Write them down in the evening to reinforce a positive perspective.

Day 10: Integrate and Reflect

Review the week, noting which practices felt most effective and sustainable. Choose the tools you will continue using for ongoing support.

Each step in this plan builds on previous practices, fostering steady progress without overwhelming demands. The following sections describe the foundational tools included throughout the plan in detail.

Daily Grounding Techniques

Calm requires active cultivation through intentional habits, not just the absence of stress. Grounding techniques consist of brief activities that direct your attention away from intrusive thoughts and anchor it in the present. Three primary techniques form the foundation of a daily calm practice: deep breathing, sensory focus, and body scans.

1. **Deep Breathing**

   Intentional breathing signals the nervous system to slow down. Practicing this regularly provides a reliable method to manage emotional overwhelm.

   To practice deep breathing, sit upright with both feet on the floor. Inhale for a count of four, hold for four, and exhale slowly for six to eight counts. Repeat this process for three to five cycles, observing the sensation of your breath moving in and out of your body. Use this technique:

   - Upon waking, before using your phone
   - When transitioning between work tasks
   - When you notice tension or racing thoughts

2. **Sensory Focus**

   Anxiety often pulls the mind away from the present moment. Sensory focus brings attention back by using physical sensations. Choose one sense, sight, sound, touch, taste, or smell, and for three minutes, observe it closely.

   - The colors and light in your surroundings

- The sensation of your chair, clothing, or air on your skin
- The background sounds in your environment

Do not analyze your observations. Notice them, allow them, and gently redirect your focus if your mind wanders.

3. **Body Scans**

   Body scans address the physical manifestations of anxiety. Lie down or sit comfortably, close your eyes, and mentally check in with each part of your body, starting from your toes and moving upward. Notice areas of tension or comfort without trying to change them. This process can:

   - Reduce unconscious muscular tension
   - Strengthen the connection between mental and physical awareness
   - Prepare your body for deeper relaxation before sleep

Using these techniques, either in rotation or as needed, helps you recognize early signals of stress.

Journaling Prompts to Untangle Thoughts

Journaling provides a structured way to explore your internal experiences and connect them with your external reality. By putting your thoughts on paper, you can interrupt repetitive mental patterns and nurture self-compassion. Even brief, intentional writing sessions can offer clarity and relief from persistent overthinking.

To keep the process manageable, use clear and concise prompts. Focus on expressing your thoughts directly instead of producing long narratives. The following five-minute evening prompts offer practical support to help you process your thoughts. You can use these prompts repeatedly or rotate them during a ten-day period:

- *What thoughts recurred most today? Did any seem exaggerated or disproportionate?*
- *If I put aside worries about outcomes, what would I choose to focus on right now?*
- *Where did I notice physical tension today, and what thoughts accompanied it?*
- *What is one thing I handled better today compared to yesterday, however small?*
- *What question do I wish I could release for the night?*

These prompts aim to clarify your thought patterns and help you observe them with a neutral perspective. Solving every problem is not the goal. Many high-achievers tend to analyze or critique their responses. Approach these prompts with curiosity and openness. Avoid judging or editing your reflections. By maintaining this attitude, you create a supportive environment for self-exploration and mental clarity.

Guided journaling enables you to recognize recurring thoughts, emotional responses, and behavioral patterns. When you write about your experiences, you can identify areas where your thinking becomes repetitive or where your emotions influence your actions. This awareness lays the groundwork for increased self-understanding and well-being.

Journaling with these prompts can become a practical tool for anyone seeking to manage overthinking, reduce stress, and build self-compassion. The practice encourages you to notice your thoughts without becoming entangled in them. By observing your internal experiences and reflecting on your day, you gain insight into your mental and emotional habits. This process supports a clearer mind and greater resilience in facing daily challenges.

Morning and Evening Rituals for Setting Intentions

Intentional rituals provide structure and establish clear boundaries for your thoughts. By starting and ending your day with brief, purposeful actions, you can avoid slipping into mental autopilot and gain greater control over your focus and mindset.

Morning Ritual

Set the tone for your day with a concise intention-setting routine. Upon waking, avoid checking emails or messages immediately. Instead, pause and ask yourself, "What is one quality I want to bring into today?" This quality could be patience, focus, kindness, or any attribute you wish to emphasize.

Take three slow, deliberate breaths. As you breathe, visualize yourself navigating the day while consistently embodying your chosen quality. Reinforce this intention by writing it on a sticky note or in your planner, making it visible as a reminder throughout your day.

This simple practice helps redirect your mind away from habitual worries and toward purposeful presence. It can support clearer decision-making and enhance your ability to respond thoughtfully to challenges as they arise.

Evening Ritual

Conclude your day with an intentional wind-down routine that signals it is safe to release the day's events. Select a calming activity such as a body scan, gentle stretching, or reading a soothing passage. Spend one minute reflecting on something that went well or a quality you appreciate about yourself. This positive focus can foster a sense of accomplishment and self-respect.

Before sleep, review three things you are ready to let go of, such as unfinished tasks, regrets, or self-criticisms. Writing these down or mentally acknowledging them can help your mind disengage from persistent concerns, creating space for rest and renewal.

Establishing these rituals at both the beginning and end of your day trains your mind to transition intentionally between states of alertness and rest. This practice demonstrates that you have the capacity to engage with your thoughts deliberately, even when unexpected or difficult emotions surface. By marking these daily transitions, you cultivate a greater sense of agency and emotional balance.

Mindfulness Practices for Busy Schedules

Mindfulness does not require clearing your mind or spending lengthy periods in meditation. You can achieve meaningful results with brief, targeted pauses throughout your day, even during demanding times.

Integrate mindfulness into your routine using these practical strategies:

- ***One-Minute Pause***: When you wait for a meeting to start or a web page to load, spend one minute observing five things in your environment. Focus on what you see without judgment, allowing your attention to settle in the present moment.
- ***Mindful Movement***: As you walk to your car, down the hall, or pace during a phone call, direct your attention to the rhythm of your steps and the physical

sensations in your body. Notice how your body moves and feels with each step.

- ***Noticing Cues***: Let routine moments, such as waiting for coffee to brew, standing by the elevator, or brushing your teeth, prompt you to notice your breath and posture. Use these intervals as reminders to reconnect with your body and breathing.
- ***Grounding Object***: Carry a small item, such as a smooth stone, a piece of jewelry, or a textured keychain. When you need to refocus, touch this object and bring your awareness to its texture and weight. This practice helps you return to the present moment.

Consistently engaging in these micro-practices helps reclaim moments that might otherwise slip into automatic rumination. By training your attention in this way, you promote a sense of calm and presence, even during the busiest days.

This ten-day program focuses on experimentation, awareness, and habit-building at a manageable pace. Racing thoughts may continue on some days. The goal is not to eliminate them but to respond with clarity and intention.

Combining breathing exercises, sensory grounding, mindful pauses, and short reflection periods creates a daily rhythm that supports nervous system regulation and mental flexibility. Journaling gives persistent worries a structured outlet, which reduces their pull on attention. Morning and evening rituals frame the day with purpose.

At the end of each ten-day cycle, review which practices felt natural and which required more effort. Adjust them to fit your schedule and needs. The habits developed during these first ten days prepare you for deeper boundary work and greater clarity, supporting a shift away from anxious autopilot and toward a more grounded, present state of mind.

Strengthening Emotional Boundaries: Days 11–20

After establishing a foundation of calm and self-awareness in the first ten days, the next step involves fortifying your emotional boundaries. For high-achieving women, the ability to define and protect these boundaries is transformative. In this chapter, you'll learn what emotional boundaries are, recognize your own limits and triggers, develop assertive communication skills, and practice setting firm boundaries in both personal and professional relationships. Each day will include reflection activities so these practices become instinctive and sustainable over time.

Defining Emotional Boundaries and Understanding Their Importance

Emotional boundaries are invisible lines that distinguish your feelings, needs, and responsibilities from those of others. They help you maintain your individual identity while you offer empathy or support to those around you. Clear emotional boundaries prevent you from taking on unnecessary emotional labor, feeling accountable for others' moods, or letting external pressures determine your self-worth.

Emotional boundaries are particularly important for high-achieving women. Without them, you may overcommit, absorb stress from colleagues or family, and neglect your own needs. Many high-functioning women instinctively manage others' problems or fulfill unspoken expectations, sometimes sacrificing their own well-being. Boundaries do not prevent you from caring for others; instead, they provide a healthy structure that allows you to support others without compromising your identity or depleting your energy.

Recognizing Personal Limits and Emotional Triggers

Understanding your personal limits is essential for establishing effective boundaries. Begin by identifying where your boundaries lie and when you are most susceptible to having them crossed. This self-awareness enables you to take proactive measures to protect your well-being. Pay close attention to your emotional responses in various settings. Emotions such as resentment, guilt, overwhelm, or anxiety can indicate that someone has tested or violated your boundaries.

Several warning signs suggest you have reached or exceeded your limits. You may feel pressured to agree to requests when you would prefer to say no. Dread before specific interactions or events often signals discomfort with your current boundaries. Certain meetings or conversations may leave you feeling depleted or exhausted. Persistent frustration or irritability, especially with particular individuals, can point to boundary issues. You may also notice that you are ignoring your own needs or neglecting your personal goals in favor of others' expectations.

Emotional triggers can stem from external sources, such as a coworker assigning you extra work, or from internal habits, like avoiding conflict or seeking approval. Recognizing these signals gives you the ability to intervene early and safeguard your emotional health. When you identify the situations, people, or behaviors that trigger strong emotional reactions, you gain more control over your responses and can set clearer boundaries.

To pinpoint areas where your boundaries need reinforcement, use an emotional boundary log for Days 11 to 13. After each interaction, briefly record any strong emotions you experience and note what aspects of the exchange felt uncomfortable or draining. This systematic documentation will reveal patterns and identify specific situations or individuals that challenge your boundaries.

Reviewing these records helps you determine where to fortify your limits and take targeted action to support your emotional well-being. By consistently monitoring your emotions and responses, you develop insight into your boundary needs and can make informed decisions to protect your mental and emotional health.

Scripts and Assertive Communication Techniques

Once you identify your limits and triggers, communicate your boundaries clearly and confidently. Assertive communication is essential for this process. It means expressing your needs and preferences directly and honestly, while maintaining respect for others. For women in demanding roles, assertiveness can sometimes be misinterpreted as harshness, making clarity and professionalism critical. The aim is to create clear and respectful dialogue that supports mutual understanding.

Effective assertive communication includes several core techniques:

- Use "I" statements. Start with phrases like "I feel," "I need," or "I am not able to." Focusing on your own experience reduces the risk of sounding accusatory or assigning blame.
- Be concise and specific. Clearly state what you need or cannot accept. Skip lengthy explanations or unnecessary justifications for your decisions or feelings.
- Maintain a calm, firm tone. A steady voice conveys confidence and ensures your message remains unambiguous.

- Use positive framing when possible. Phrase requests in a way that signals mutual respect and cooperation, while keeping your boundaries intact.

Prepared scripts help make these conversations less intimidating. Practicing with templates allows you to build confidence in expressing your needs. Use these examples as a starting point:

- *"I understand this is important, but I am not able to take on additional responsibilities at this time."*
- *"I need to end our meeting at 3:00 as planned so I can keep my schedule on track."*
- *"I feel overwhelmed when there are last-minute changes. Can we agree on more notice in the future?"*
- *"Thank you for thinking of me, but I won't be able to participate."*

Dedicate Days 14 and 15 to practicing these scripts in low-pressure situations. Rehearse with a trusted friend or use a journal to write out your responses. Repeat the scripts aloud until they feel and sound natural. This practice will prepare you to communicate your boundaries effectively, even when you face pressure or challenging situations. Consistent rehearsal ensures your assertive communication feels authentic and professional in any context

Setting Boundaries in Professional and Personal Relationships

Boundary-setting takes distinct forms in professional and personal contexts, but the underlying principles remain consistent. In the workplace, clear boundaries help prevent burnout and support productivity. In personal relationships, they foster respect and individual growth.

In professional settings, define your responsibilities and limits during project meetings. Decline non-essential requests by referencing your current priorities or workload. Protect your personal time by disabling work notifications outside of business hours. If a colleague repeatedly disregards your boundaries, restate them and communicate the impact. For example, say, "When deadlines change at the last minute, it affects my ability to produce quality work. Let's establish a process that ensures more consistency."

In personal relationships, express your emotional needs directly. For instance, say, "I need some quiet time this evening to recharge." Address recurring boundary concerns promptly and calmly, instead of allowing frustration to accumulate. Set clear expectations with those close to you, especially regarding communication, involvement in decisions, or shared activities. Decline invitations or favors that drain your energy, prioritizing meaningful connections over quantity.

You do not owe lengthy explanations for your boundaries. If someone challenges your boundaries, restate your needs calmly and clearly. People may resist, particularly if they expect you to overextend yourself. Consistent communication and follow-through will help shift these dynamics and reinforce your boundaries.

Effective boundary-setting supports well-being and healthier relationships both at work and at home. By clarifying your limits, communicating assertively, and responding to pushback with consistency, you create an environment where your needs and commitments receive proper respect.

Daily Reflection Activities to Reinforce Boundary Habits

To make boundary-setting automatic, incorporate daily reflection into your routine. Self-reflection increases awareness, helping you recognize lapses and celebrate successes in enforcing limits.

During Days 16–20, practice these activities:

- ***Morning intention***: Begin the day by choosing one boundary to uphold. For example, pause before agreeing to new requests.
- ***Evening review***: Reflect on your interactions. Note where you maintained boundaries and where

improvement is needed. Write a short summary for clarity.

- ***Boundary wins journal***: Record every instance of enforcing a limit, even small ones. Tracking progress builds confidence.
- ***What-ifs exercise***: Mentally rehearse upcoming situations where your boundaries may be challenged. Practice how you will respond.
- ***Self-compassion check-in***: At the end of the day, remind yourself that boundary work can feel uncomfortable. Focus on consistency rather than perfection.

As these exercises become part of your routine, you will recognize patterns in your behavior and observe your successes grow. Acknowledge every instance of progress. Effective boundaries develop through regular practice and reflection. Daily reflection supports skill development and helps boundary-setting become a natural habit.

Building emotional boundaries begins with an honest assessment of your feelings and limits, followed by clear and compassionate communication, and reinforced through consistent practice. The exercises and strategies in this chapter are meant to help you turn boundary-setting into tangible actions, so you can safeguard your time, energy, and well-being.

As you complete this section and work toward regaining mental clarity, keep in mind that strong boundaries do not push others away. Instead, they affirm your right to thrive according to your own needs. Every effort you make to strengthen these boundaries contributes to lasting calm, effectiveness, and self-assurance.

Restoring Mental Clarity: Days 21–30

The final ten days of your 30-day guide mark a shift toward renewal and refinement. After grounding yourself in calm and building strong emotional boundaries, now is the time to restore true mental clarity. This process is not about simply emptying your mind; it's about consciously creating space for what matters, managing your attention with intention, and developing sustainable habits that support clear thinking and confident decision-making. The strategies in this chapter will help you cut through the mental clutter that accumulates so easily in a high-achieving life.

Strategies for Decluttering Mental Space

High-functioning anxiety often produces mental congestion. Persistent thoughts, overflowing to-do lists, and constant worry occupy mental energy and reduce focus. Intentionally decluttering your mind helps create clarity and emotional ease. Structured strategies allow you to regain control over your inner space and reduce the strain of continuous mental activity.

Perform a daily mental "dump"

Dedicate ten minutes in the evening or during a lunch break to write down all lingering thoughts, worries, reminders, and tasks. Use a notebook or digital document, and write freely without filtering. Transfer everything from your mind onto paper, from minor errands to larger responsibilities or concerns. This exercise separates thoughts from your immediate awareness, reduces rumination, and provides a tangible record of items you can manage later.

Review your commitments and responsibilities

Examine ongoing obligations and projects to determine which align with your current priorities. Identify tasks that no longer serve your goals and remove, delegate, or postpone them. Small adjustments, such as delaying a non-urgent task, unsubscribing from emails or newsletters, or reducing low-priority activities, can free mental bandwidth. Streamlining commitments prevents unnecessary stress and allows you to focus on what matters most.

Audit the information sources that occupy your attention

Evaluate how often you check work emails, social media, or news updates, especially outside scheduled hours. Decide which sources provide genuine value and which create mental noise. Establish designated periods for consuming information and avoid habitual checking that interrupts focus. Limiting exposure to distracting or low-value content reduces mental clutter and strengthens attention for important tasks.

Intentional mental decluttering strengthens clarity and resilience. Organizing thoughts, streamlining obligations, and managing attention create cognitive space for reflection, problem-solving, and calm. These strategies support focus, reduce overwhelm, and improve overall well-being, allowing you to approach daily challenges with steadiness and presence.

Prioritization and Intentional Time Management

After decluttering your mental space, focus on what truly requires your attention. High-achieving women often juggle multiple priorities at once. Constant urgency can fragment attention and reduce clarity. Intentional prioritization directs mental energy toward meaningful tasks instead of reacting to every demand.

Select your top three priorities each day

Begin by identifying the tasks that will move you closer to your personal or professional goals or provide the most sense of accomplishment and peace of mind. Avoid long to-do lists that can overwhelm your focus. List three essential tasks for the day, choose two secondary items to address if time allows, and identify one task, worry, or minor responsibility to release. This framework promotes disciplined progress and protects attention from distraction.

Align your calendar with your priorities

Reserve uninterrupted blocks for complex or meaningful work. For example, dedicate the first hour after your morning routine for focused effort or set aside a brief period in the afternoon for administrative tasks. Use digital tools, a paper planner, or both to reinforce consistent practice. The method is less important than the habit of regular scheduling.

Practice saying no strategically

Evaluate new commitments carefully. Accept only tasks that align with current objectives and well-being. Declining obligations that do not serve your priorities strengthens control over your time and energy and supports mental clarity.

Intentional time management and prioritization build a structured foundation for productivity and calm. Focusing on essential tasks, matching your schedule to priorities, and protecting your time from unnecessary obligations reduces mental clutter. This approach allows energy to flow toward meaningful work, enhances focus, and reinforces steady progress while maintaining well-being.

Focus-Enhancing Exercises and Mini Digital Detoxes

Sharpen mental clarity by training your brain to focus and disengage from distracting stimuli. During days 21 to 30, incorporate targeted exercises and brief digital detox periods to refresh your mind and strengthen attention.

- ***Single-tasking***: Choose one activity and devote 20 to 30 minutes of undivided attention to it. Silence notifications and set a visible timer. When your mind begins to wander, gently bring focus back to the task. This practice strengthens concentration and helps you maintain presence in the moment.
- ***Mindful observation***: Spend several minutes closely observing your environment, a cup of tea, or bodily sensations. Notice small details and subtle changes, such as sounds, colors, or textures. Mindful observation anchors awareness in the present moment, reduces mental chatter, and fosters clarity.
- ***Short, guided meditations***: Use meditations designed to enhance focus, available through apps or recordings. Even five-minute sessions can recalibrate attention and provide a mental reset. Repeated practice trains the mind to sustain concentration over longer periods.
- ***Mini digital detoxes***: Schedule short, device-free periods during your day. Avoid phone or screen use for 20 minutes after waking or designate lunch breaks as screen-free. Refrain from multitasking with digital devices so your mind can engage fully with tasks or surroundings.
- ***Extended weekly digital break***: Choose one evening per week for a longer period without devices. Stop

using email, social media, or streaming platforms at a set hour. Use the time for analog activities, such as reading a physical book, journaling, or engaging in creative hobbies. These alternatives provide stimulation without digital input and reinforce mental stillness.

Consistent practice of these exercises reduces digital fatigue, clears mental clutter, and strengthens attention. Cultivating focus through these methods supports productivity, clarity, and a sense of calm.

Regular Self-Check-ins to Reassess Clarity

Busy schedules can easily result in mental clutter, making it important to maintain clarity through regular self-check-ins. Establishing this habit involves taking brief, intentional pauses to observe your mental state, assess your focus, and make necessary adjustments to your actions.

Set aside a few quiet minutes at consistent times, such as at the end of the day or after lunch. Use this time to answer the following questions:

- *Am I feeling focused and grounded, or scattered and reactive?*
- *Is my mind preoccupied with worries or replaying previous conversations?*

- *Do my recent activities and priorities align with what matters most to me?*
- *What can I let go of today to create more mental space?*

Respond honestly to each question. As you reflect, notice patterns in your thoughts and behaviors. Pay attention to specific moments or types of interactions that tend to disrupt your focus. Use these insights to modify your environment or approach so you can sustain greater clarity.

When you identify resistance, consider whether you are maintaining certain worries or tasks out of habit or obligation. Clearly recognizing these tendencies allows you to begin addressing and releasing them. For example:

- List recurring worries and evaluate whether they serve a constructive purpose.
- Examine tasks you frequently postpone or complete out of routine. Decide if they remain relevant to your goals.
- Identify environmental factors that contribute to distraction, such as excessive notifications or interruptions.
- Adjust your schedule or workspace to support periods of uninterrupted focus.

Practicing regular self-check-ins promotes self-awareness and encourages a more deliberate, focused approach to daily responsibilities. By making this practice a consistent part of your routine, you can manage mental clutter more effectively and ensure your actions align with your priorities.

Templates for Daily and Weekly Review Sessions

Structured reflection supports progress during the final ten days. Simple templates help you track what enhances focus and what causes mental clutter.

Daily Review Template (5 minutes each evening):

- List your top three priorities for the day. Indicate if you completed them. If not, specify the obstacles encountered.
- Record any unexpected distractions or sources of mental clutter.
- Note one insight gained from the day, such as when you focus best or what increases your stress.
- Identify one item to release, like a specific worry, a perfectionistic standard, or a nonessential task.

Weekly Review Template (15 to 20 minutes at week's end):

- List actions or habits that supported mental space and clarity this week.
- Identify distractions or sources of overwhelm that resurfaced.

- Evaluate if your priorities matched your actual goals and values.
- Determine which boundaries or decluttering practices to reinforce in the upcoming week.
- Set three intentions for the coming week, such as maintaining digital-free evenings or declining new tasks that do not align with your current focus.

Keep these templates simple and accessible in a notebook, planner, or digital note. Consistent reflection increases awareness and strengthens the habit of maintaining mental clarity.

The final third of your 30-day program focuses on managing your mental environment as intentionally as your physical space. By clearing mental clutter, prioritizing deliberately, sharpening focus, and scheduling regular self-check-ins, you restore clarity and build resilience against future overwhelm. The routines and templates from these ten days serve as practical tools you can return to whenever needed, making clarity a sustainable habit rather than a temporary goal.

These strategies help you recognize and remove mental clutter before it accumulates, creating space for calm attention and creative thinking. Your mind, previously stretched by constant demands and overcommitment, gains room to focus, reflect, and perform at its best. The next chapter provides guidance on integrating these practices into daily routines to maintain ongoing calm and balance.

Mastering Daily Routines for Ongoing Calm

ily routine serves as a powerful tool for maintaining calm, particularly in the fast-paced lives of high-achieving women. While relaxation techniques offer short-term relief, lasting balance comes from days structured with intention. This chapter provides practical guidance, including sample routines, targeted habits, and evidence-based strategies, to help you design a daily rhythm that reduces anxiety and fosters mental clarity.

Sample Daily Routines for Sustained Balance

Developing a daily routine is not about achieving perfection. The focus lies in consistency and sustainability. Instead of filling your schedule with a long list of tasks, identify core practices that anchor your day, no matter how busy or unpredictable it becomes.

Consider including these elements in a calm-seeking routine:

- ***Morning grounding***: Start your day with five minutes of deep breathing, gentle stretching, or a short mindfulness session. This practice centers your mind before engaging with email, news, or social interactions.

- ***Focus block***: Reserve a specific time for your most mentally demanding task, aiming for a distraction-free environment, even if only for 30 minutes.
- ***Intentional breaks***: Take two to three short breaks during the workday for mindful walking, enjoying a healthy snack, or writing down persistent worries. These breaks support mental reset and prevent burnout.
- ***Evening wind-down***: As the workday ends, create a clear transition between work and rest. Engage in calming activities such as reading, journaling, or taking a warm shower. Avoid screens for at least 30 minutes before bedtime to promote better sleep quality.
- ***Nightly reflection***: Spend a few minutes documenting successes, frustrations, and unresolved thoughts. This habit closes mental loops that can contribute to anxiety and supports restful sleep.

Routine structure will vary according to individual lifestyles and responsibilities, but these core components offer a strong foundation. Repeating these elements daily builds stability and resilience. Flexibility ensures your routine adapts to changing demands while continuing to support your sense of calm.

Sleep Hygiene and Mindful Mornings

Restful sleep forms the foundation of calm and resilience. High-functioning anxiety often disrupts sleep, causing racing thoughts at night or early awakenings. Improving sleep hygiene supports mental stability and emotional regulation. Clear, practical steps can help establish a healthier sleep routine and a focused start to the day.

To promote restful, restorative sleep, follow these practices:

- Maintain a consistent bedtime and wake-up time, including on weekends. This supports your body's natural rhythms and improves sleep quality.
- Reserve your bedroom for sleep and quiet reading. Keep work materials and electronic screens out of the space to help your brain associate the room with rest.
- Avoid caffeine after mid-afternoon and refrain from eating heavy meals close to bedtime. This reduces the risk of sleep disturbances.
- Dim lights and reduce noise as bedtime approaches. These cues signal your brain to begin winding down for the night.

Preparation for quality sleep begins before you get into bed. The first moments after waking also play a critical role in shaping your mindset for the day. Instead of immediately engaging with devices or responding to messages, adopt morning habits that foster focus and calm.

Start your morning with these steps:

- Drink a full glass of water to rehydrate and signal the beginning of the day.
- Step outside or open a window to expose yourself to natural light, which resets your internal clock and enhances mood.
- Select one centering activity, such as meditative breathing, repeating an affirmation, or reviewing a daily intention, to anchor your mindset.

A consistent sleep-wake cycle and mindful morning routine do not require extra time but depend on intentional choices that prioritize mental well-being. Implementing these strategies can help manage anxiety and contribute to greater resilience throughout the day.

Physical Activity and Nutrition for Brain Health

Physical and mental well-being are interconnected. Consistent movement and proper nutrition support reduced anxiety and improved cognitive clarity. However, busy schedules often result in neglecting these essential habits.

For physical activity, prioritize consistency. Lengthy workouts are not required to achieve benefits. Aim for at least 20 minutes of moderate movement on most days of the week. Activities such as brisk walking, cycling, stretching, or dancing at home help release endorphins, reduce muscular tension, and improve mental focus.

Structured exercise provides several benefits:

- Lowers stress hormones such as cortisol
- Improves sleep quality and increases energy
- Supports executive function and memory

Nutrition also plays a crucial role in maintaining brain health. The foods you choose impact your body, decision-making, emotional regulation, and concentration. Strive for balanced meals that include:

- Lean proteins, such as chicken, eggs, or legumes
- Complex carbohydrates from whole grains and vegetables
- Healthy fats from nuts, olive oil, or avocados
- Hydrating fluids like water or herbal teas

Limiting sugary snacks and processed foods helps prevent blood sugar spikes and crashes, which can intensify anxiety and irritability. Regular, balanced meals help stabilize blood sugar levels, supporting mood and cognitive function.

Developing a routine for physical activity and mindful eating enhances both mental and physical health. By focusing on consistency and balanced nutrition, you can support sharper focus, emotional stability, and overall well-being.

Scheduling "Worry Windows" to Contain Overthinking

High-functioning anxiety often appears as a constant stream of worry that disrupts focus and rest. Left unchecked, it can lead to restlessness and clouded thinking.

"Worry windows" provide a structured way to manage these thoughts. Rather than trying to eliminate worry, you confine it to a brief, intentional period. This helps preserve focus, maintain productivity, and support emotional balance.

To implement worry windows:

- Select a specific daily time slot, such as 15 minutes after lunch or before you leave work.
- Keep a notebook available to record worries that arise outside your chosen window. When a concern surfaces, make a note to address it during the scheduled time.
- During the worry window, review your list, analyze each concern, and consider possible solutions. When the time ends, close the notebook and shift your attention to restorative activities.

This approach trains your mind to link worry with a designated period, reducing intrusive thoughts throughout the day. Scheduled worry sessions allow more energy for tasks and other priorities. By setting boundaries around worry, you protect mental clarity and reduce emotional fatigue. Regular use of worry windows provides a practical, sustainable tool for managing anxiety.

Habit Tracking for Ongoing Progress

Building and maintaining new routines requires visibility and accountability. Habit tracking provides a clear measure of commitment, a visual record of progress, and actionable feedback for refining your practices.

Tracking can be simple or advanced. A basic tracker might be a calendar where you mark each day you complete a grounding exercise, evening routine, or workout. Digital apps can prompt you, tally streaks, and analyze patterns.

To use habit tracking effectively:

- ***Select a few key habits to monitor***. Focusing on a limited number prevents overwhelm and increases the likelihood of success.
- ***Define what counts as a win***. For example, determine if spending five minutes on a morning routine meets your goal.
- ***Review your tracker weekly***. If a habit is frequently missed, identify obstacles. Adjust timing, break it into smaller steps, or link it to an existing routine.
- ***Celebrate consistency***. Recognize streaks regardless of length. Treat setbacks as information to guide

adjustments. The aim is sustained improvement, not perfect execution.

Tracking habits turns maintenance into an active process. It helps you see which routines anchor your day, which require modification, and where extra support or self-compassion is needed. Clear metrics and regular reflection make habit tracking a practical tool for ongoing growth.

Mastering daily routines for calm requires combining small, purposeful actions. Morning practices set the tone for mindful engagement. Movement and nutrition fuel your focus. Worry windows declutter your thoughts, and habit tracking keeps you on course.

Days will come when your structure falters or challenges arise. These routines act as resilient anchors. They are flexible, supportive, and sustaining. Over time, practices shift from task completion to self-support, reinforcing the clarity and balance developed earlier.

With these foundations, you can maintain calm and respond to triggers with confidence and perspective. This prepares you for the next chapter on handling setbacks.

Navigating Triggers and Setbacks

Even the most thoughtfully constructed routines and carefully crafted plans will encounter turbulence. For high-achieving women managing high-functioning anxiety, setbacks do not represent failure; they are a natural part of personal growth. Triggers, stressful situations, and occasional boundary breaches will occur. Your response and ability to recalibrate play a crucial role in maintaining progress and restoring calm.

Identifying Common Setbacks and High-Risk Situations

Awareness is essential for effectively navigating setbacks, particularly for high-achieving women managing high-functioning anxiety. Recognizing and anticipating situations that challenge composure allows you to create concrete strategies for response. While individual triggers vary, several high-risk situations frequently appear in this population.

1. ***Overcommitment***: Accepting multiple responsibilities to meet high standards or please others can overwhelm coping abilities. Overcommitment often leads to chronic stress, difficulty prioritizing, and neglect of personal needs. This cycle can result in burnout and reduced performance.

2. ***Disruptions to Routine***: Unplanned demands such as last-minute meetings, family emergencies, or unexpected travel interfere with established habits. These interruptions make it harder to maintain self-care practices and increase feelings of anxiety.
3. ***High-Pressure Performance Events***: Presentations, looming deadlines, and evaluations often generate intense self-criticism and overthinking. The desire to excel can amplify anxiety and reduce confidence in abilities.
4. ***Criticism, Conflict, or Perceived Failures***: Negative feedback, misunderstandings, or interpersonal conflict may trigger self-doubt. These scenarios often lead to rumination about past interactions and heightened emotional distress.
5. ***Social Overload***: Attending numerous social events or continuous networking without downtime can deplete emotional energy. Lack of boundaries in social situations may cause exhaustion and blur personal and professional distinctions.
6. ***Fatigue and Insufficient Self-Care***: Poor sleep, skipped meals, and lack of breaks reduce resilience and increase susceptibility to anxiety. Chronic fatigue undermines the ability to cope effectively with everyday challenges.

Steps to Identify Personal High-Risk Situations

- Observe reactions in different environments, conversations, and tasks. Note situations that consistently increase discomfort or trigger unhelpful coping.
- Record details in a journal, including context, emotional responses, and subsequent behaviors.
- Review notes to reveal patterns, focusing on recurring situations, people, or themes linked to spikes in anxiety.
- Develop strategies to manage future setbacks, such as limiting social commitments or scheduling breaks during high-pressure periods.
- Apply these strategies consistently to strengthen self-awareness, resilience, and boundary maintenance.

Systematic monitoring of experiences and responses empowers proactive self-management, helping maintain well-being even under pressure.

Adaptive Coping Strategies Without Self-Judgment

When setbacks occur, respond with understanding instead of criticism. Adaptive coping involves recognizing what happened and taking steps to stabilize yourself. Avoid self-blame or focusing repeatedly on mistakes. This approach supports emotional balance and allows forward movement in a constructive way.

Follow these steps to respond adaptively:

1. **Pause and Notice**

   Take several slow, deep breaths before reacting.

   This interrupts automatic self-criticism and creates space for a thoughtful response.

2. **Reframe the Situation**

   Recognize that setbacks offer opportunities to learn and practice new skills.

   Understand that a single setback does not define your abilities or value.

3. **Use Grounding Techniques**

   Focus on physical sensations, such as feeling the floor beneath your feet.

   Identify three things you can see in your environment.

   Practice a calming breath exercise to anchor yourself in the present.

4. **Create a Reset Ritual**

   Engage in a brief activity that shifts your focus and clears your mind.

   Examples include taking a short walk, splashing cold water on your face, or listening to a favorite music track.

5. **Practice Immediate Self-Compassion**

   Speak to yourself with kindness, as you would to a friend facing difficulty.

   Use supportive statements such as, "It's okay to have a tough moment. I can choose my next step."

Setbacks and difficult emotions do not determine the outcome of your day. Practicing adaptive coping builds resilience and reinforces your ability to respond with intention. Discomfort is temporary, and you maintain the capacity to handle challenges without harsh self-judgment. Consistent use of these strategies strengthens your emotional well-being, fosters a healthier relationship with yourself, and equips you to manage stress in a balanced, effective manner.

Troubleshooting Boundary Breaches and Managing Stress Spikes

Maintaining boundaries requires noticing when they have been crossed and responding effectively. Stress spikes often indicate that personal limits have been exceeded, whether due to others or your own choices. Recognizing these moments and taking deliberate action helps preserve well-being and professional relationships.

Follow these steps to address boundary breaches:

1. **Recognize the Breach**

   Monitor your mood, energy, and internal dialogue for shifts that signal discomfort.

   Notice physical cues such as jaw tension, muscle tightness, or racing thoughts.

   Observe situations that trigger frustration, fatigue, or resentment.

2. **Pause Before Reacting**

   Create a brief gap between the event and your response.

   Avoid rushing to appease others or smooth over the situation.

   Use this time to check in with yourself and determine your needs.

3. **Clarify What Happened**

   Ask questions to identify the problem:

- *Did you agree to something against your judgment?*
- *Did you ignore a comment that needed addressing?*
- *Are you accepting responsibilities beyond your capacity?*

Pinpointing the issue guides an appropriate response.

4. **Choose and Communicate Your Response**

Decide how to reassert your boundary using clear, respectful language.

Example statements include:

- "I have taken on too much and need to step back."
- "That comment felt unfair, and I need to address it."

If immediate resolution is not possible, plan a follow-up, such as scheduling a conversation or sending a written message.

5. **Restore Your Energy**

Engage in self-care to regulate your nervous system.

Effective actions include stretching, deep breathing, walking outside, or finding a quiet space.

During sudden stress spikes, use grounding techniques to maintain composure: press your feet firmly into the floor, repeat a calming phrase such as "This will pass," and maintain steady, controlled breaths.

Consistent application of these strategies reinforces personal limits, supports measured responses, and builds resilience in both personal and professional settings.

When and How to Seek External Support

Recognizing when to seek external support plays a critical role in maintaining mental health and overall well-being. Relying solely on internal coping strategies may not always prove effective, especially when facing repeated or intensified setbacks. Seeking help demonstrates resilience and self-awareness. Understanding the specific signs that indicate a need for assistance helps you maintain your functioning at work, at home, and in relationships.

You may benefit from external support if you notice any of the following:

- Setbacks or triggers occur more frequently or with greater intensity, making it harder to manage your usual responsibilities.
- Anxiety or stress reactions interfere with performance at work, disrupt home life, or negatively affect relationships with others.

- You feel trapped in unhelpful patterns and cannot change your responses, despite making conscious efforts to adapt.

You experience isolation or find it challenging to share your feelings with people you trust.

Seeking support does not indicate weakness. Instead, it reflects a proactive approach to managing your well-being. Early intervention can prevent stress from escalating and reduce the risk of more serious mental health issues.

Effective Strategies for Seeking Support

To maximize the benefits of external support, consider the following strategies:

- Act as soon as you recognize warning signs rather than waiting until stress becomes overwhelming. Early action helps you address problems before they reach a crisis point.
- Initiate a direct and honest conversation with a trusted friend, family member, or mentor. Begin by stating your needs clearly. For instance, you might say:
    - "I need help talking this through."
    - "Could you help me brainstorm some solutions?"
    - "Can you check in with me this week?"

- Communicate your needs specifically. This allows others to understand how best to support you and enables them to respond effectively.
- Remain open to different forms of support. Sometimes, practical assistance such as help with daily tasks can be as valuable as emotional encouragement.

If you continue to experience anxiety or setbacks that disrupt your well-being or daily functioning, professional assistance may be appropriate. Consider these options:

- Consult a licensed counselor or therapist. Mental health professionals can provide structured, evidence-based tools tailored to your unique situation, helping you develop new coping strategies and address underlying issues.
- Join community groups, online forums, or workshops focused on anxiety, boundaries, or related topics. These groups connect you with peers who share similar experiences, offering insight, encouragement, and practical advice.
- Explore support networks within your workplace or educational institution. Employee assistance programs, campus counseling centers, or peer mentoring networks can provide confidential resources and guidance.

By recognizing when you need external support and implementing effective strategies to seek it, you strengthen your resilience and protect your mental health. Clear communication and a willingness to seek help ensure that you maintain your well-being and continue to function effectively in all areas of your life.

Encouraging Resilience with Positive Self-Talk

Resilience involves the ability to recover, adapt, and progress despite setbacks or anxiety. Positive self-talk serves as a practical tool to reinforce this adaptive mindset.

Effective self-talk does not ignore reality or promote constant self-cheerleading. Aim for realistic optimism by balancing empathy for your experience with reminders of your capability. Several approaches can support this process:

- Use affirming language. Instead of saying, "I always mess up boundaries," try, "I am learning to notice when my boundaries need adjusting."
- Validate your emotions. Permit yourself to experience frustration, overwhelm, or disappointment without suppressing those feelings.
- Recall prior successes. Identify a specific moment when you navigated a difficult week or reset after a challenge. Use that memory to counter negative self-talk.
- Prepare situational mantras. Identify short phrases to use in stressful moments, such as "I can choose to

pause" or "This is difficult, but I have managed before."

Write several sentences that resonate with you and display them in your workspace, journal, or phone. Repeated exposure to these statements helps reinforce adaptive thinking patterns and strengthens your internal support system during high-anxiety periods.

Setbacks and triggers provide opportunities to refine coping tools and practice new responses. Each challenging moment offers feedback on where boundaries require reinforcement, which strategies work best, and when to seek additional support.

Focus on your capacity to adjust and recover. Analyze factors leading to the setback, apply self-compassion, and identify a clear next step. This process supports resilience rooted in awareness, adaptive action, and effective self-talk. Consistent application of these steps promotes steady progress, regardless of how many times you need to recalibrate.

As you continue building a calmer and more focused life, view setbacks as opportunities for growth instead of sources of shame. The next chapter explores how to integrate external support into your journey, further strengthening your foundation for sustained calm and clarity.

Building a Support System

Building a strong support system is essential for sustaining progress in managing high-functioning anxiety. While internal work such as identifying triggers, establishing routines, and setting boundaries forms the foundation, positive external relationships play a critical role. Meaningful connections provide encouragement, perspective, accountability, and at times, necessary expertise. This chapter outlines practical strategies for developing and expanding a support network that meets your needs during both growth and challenge.

The Role of Accountability Partners

Many high-achieving women excel at navigating personal and professional challenges independently, drawing on self-motivation and high personal standards. While self-discipline is important, external accountability can further enhance growth and well-being. Working with an accountability partner can help transform intentions into consistent, sustainable behaviors, particularly for those managing high-functioning anxiety.

Accountability partners play several important roles:

- ***Increased follow-through***: When you share specific goals, such as maintaining healthy boundaries or prioritizing self-care, with another person, your level of commitment increases. The knowledge that someone else is invested in your progress strengthens your resolve to act on your intentions.

- ***Mutual encouragement***: Accountability partners provide emotional support during setbacks and recognize your achievements, both large and small. This mutual encouragement fosters a sense of shared progress and reduces the risk of discouragement.
- ***Objective perspective***: A partner offers honest feedback and can identify patterns you might not see yourself. They may notice when you overextend yourself, revert to people-pleasing behaviors, or become stuck in overthinking. This helps you adjust your approach before small issues escalate.
- ***Reduced isolation***: High-functioning anxiety can lead to feelings of isolation and the belief that others cannot understand your experiences. Having an accountability partner reminds you that you are not alone and creates a safe space to share challenges and successes.

To establish a productive partnership, select someone you trust. Potential partners include friends, colleagues who share similar goals, or members of a professional group. Set clear expectations for communication, check-in frequency, and the type of support you both need. For example, you might agree to provide weekly updates, collaborate on solutions to challenges, or send reminders about specific tasks.

By intentionally creating a supportive partnership, you strengthen your resilience and develop more effective strategies for managing high-functioning anxiety. A structured approach to accountability not only enhances your ability to reach your goals but also reinforces a sense of connection and shared purpose.

Finding Mentors, Coaches, or Professional Therapy

While friends and peers offer encouragement, some challenges require specialized expertise. Seeking guidance from mentors, coaches, or mental health professionals shows self-awareness and strength. Each of these resources offers distinct benefits:

- ***Mentors*** provide advice based on personal experience, helping you balance ambition with well-being. They offer perspective on complex situations and assist in refining your approach to work and life challenges. Mentors can help you identify priorities, avoid common pitfalls, and model healthy success in your field.
- ***Coaches*** focus on helping you achieve specific goals. Whether in life, career, or wellness, coaches assist with challenges such as overcommitting or difficulty delegating. They use structured frameworks, monitor your progress, and hold you accountable. Coaches

apply practical strategies to help you overcome internal barriers and support lasting change.

- ***Professional therapists*** or counselors address emotional concerns that interfere with daily functioning. If you experience anxiety, stress, or persistent emotional obstacles, a therapist can identify underlying causes and teach evidence-based coping techniques. Their training equips them to address issues beyond the expertise of friends or mentors.

When seeking support, look for mentors who model balanced success in your field, coaches with recognized certification in well-being or personal development, and therapists experienced in working with high-achieving individuals. Select professionals whose approach aligns with your personal and professional goals to maximize the benefits of their support.

Do not wait for challenges to become overwhelming. Early engagement with mentors, coaches, or mental health professionals helps you address difficulties before they escalate. Taking this step fosters growth and resilience, supporting your overall well-being and success.

Communicating Your Needs to Loved Ones

Building a support system within your close relationships begins with honest communication. High-achieving women sometimes hesitate to seek help, fearing judgment or concerns about appearing needy. However, being clear with loved ones is crucial to fostering understanding and receiving meaningful support.

Consider these practical strategies:

Identify your needs beforehand. Reflect on the kind of support you require, such as advice, a listening ear, or practical help.

- Choose a calm, appropriate time for discussions. Important conversations are more effective when everyone feels relaxed and attentive.
- Use specific language. For example, instead of saying "I'm overwhelmed," specify, "I need quiet time in the evenings to recharge," or "It helps when you ask before adding plans to my schedule."
- Express appreciation. Acknowledge and reinforce supportive actions from loved ones.
- Practice patience. It may take several conversations for others to understand your needs, so be willing to clarify as needed.

Most people want to help but may not know how. Clearly stating your boundaries and preferences enables others to support you more effectively and strengthens trust within your relationships.

Joining Communities with Shared Goals

Connecting with others who share similar goals or challenges offers validation and a sense of belonging. Communities take many forms, including professional networks, local support groups, online forums, or social clubs based on shared interests. For individuals managing high-functioning anxiety, these spaces can provide understanding, encouragement, and psychological safety.

Joining a community offers several benefits:

1. ***Shared insight***: Members exchange practical strategies and real experiences that help normalize challenges and offer useful perspectives.
2. ***Motivation through connection***: Seeing others work toward similar goals can increase commitment and persistence.
3. **Emotional support**: Open conversations with people who understand reduce isolation and self-doubt.
4. ***Relationship building***: Connections formed in goal-focused groups may lead to friendships, collaboration, or mentorship.

Choose communities that align with your interests or current priorities. Options may include a local women's group focused on well-being, a professional organization, or an online space centered on stress management for high achievers. Participate at a pace that feels comfortable.

Reading discussions, reflecting on shared experiences, or offering occasional updates can foster connection and motivation without pressure.

Engaging with a supportive community reinforces the idea that growth does not happen in isolation. Shared goals and mutual understanding create an environment that supports progress, confidence, and sustained well-being.

Expanding Your Support System Gradually

Building a strong support system takes time and intention. Expanding your network at a measured pace often leads to deeper and more reliable connections.

Use the following approach to guide this process:

1. ***Start small.*** Begin with one or two key relationships, such as an accountability partner or a trusted confidant. Focus on trust, consistency, and mutual respect before expanding further.
2. ***Assess alignment and comfort.*** After spending time in new connections, evaluate whether they feel supportive and aligned with your values. Strong support depends on depth and compatibility, not numbers.
3. ***Add support in layers.*** Once a basic structure feels stable, consider adding roles such as a mentor, coach,

or community group. As circumstances change, seek resources that match your current challenges or goals.

4. ***Accept change as part of growth***. Support needs and relationships shift over time. Periodically reflect on your network. Consider whether new perspectives would be helpful, whether some connections no longer fit your direction, or whether reconnecting with a former source of guidance could add value.

A well-developed support system provides access to encouragement, insight, and perspective when needed. Trust your judgment when deciding to reach out and when to rely on your own skills. A flexible and intentional approach allows your support network to grow alongside your personal and professional development.

Building a support system involves creating a responsive and flexible network rather than completing a fixed checklist. Each step, including working with accountability partners, seeking mentorship, communicating needs, joining communities, and expanding connections with intention, strengthens your ability to handle challenges with resilience and clarity.

Reflect on which types of support feel most relevant or beneficial right now. Set small, deliberate goals, such as contacting a potential accountability partner, arranging a conversation with a mentor, or joining a community aligned with your needs. These actions create momentum and open the door to stronger connections and sustainable growth.

High-functioning anxiety often intensifies in isolation and silence. Support systems counter this pattern by fostering connection, shared understanding, and perspective. Through consistent and thoughtful relationship-building, you continue to reinforce calm and confidence, one connection at a time.

Measuring Progress and Sustaining Growth

Your achievements in establishing routines, setting emotional boundaries, and building a support system form a strong foundation for lasting well-being. Achieving real transformation calls for regular reflection and a commitment to continual growth. Change does not follow a linear path; it involves careful assessment and flexible strategies to manage both progress and periods of stagnation. This chapter presents practical methods to monitor your development, acknowledge achievements, build knowledge, restore motivation during setbacks, and maintain long-term balance.

Tools for Self-Reflection and Tracking Emotional Shifts

Gradual progress can make it hard to detect day-to-day emotional changes. Deliberate self-reflection makes these shifts more apparent and measurable. By recording your experiences, patterns, and reactions, you clarify what strategies work and identify areas needing more focus.

Journaling serves as an effective tool for self-reflection. Keeping a daily or weekly journal allows you to document your actions and emotions, such as experiencing calmer mornings, developing a supportive inner dialogue, or pausing before reacting to stress. Use prompts that encourage emotional honesty, for example:

- *What event today triggered anxiety or provided unexpected calm?*
- *Did I set or maintain a boundary today, and what was my response?*
- *How do my responses to challenges differ from a month ago?*

Mood-tracking apps offer a visual summary of your emotional patterns. These tools let you rate your mood, note triggers, and view data in graphs or summaries. A simple spreadsheet, where you record days of high anxiety or steady confidence, can also highlight trends and progress that might be overlooked.

A regular "emotional check-in" provides further insight. Each week, rate your emotional state on a scale of 1 to 10, record your mental energy, and briefly reflect on factors influencing your highs and lows. This practice helps you adjust expectations, identify recurring patterns, and recognize incremental achievements.

Celebrating Milestones and Small Wins

High achievers often concentrate on long-term goals and overlook the meaningful progress made along the way.

Acknowledging small wins sustains motivation and reinforces positive behavioral change.

Begin by defining what counts as a win. This may include choosing rest over overwork, speaking up during a challenging conversation, or protecting personal time. Even one instance of a new habit matters. Consider creating a simple reward system that supports your values, such as taking an evening off, enjoying a favorite activity, or sharing the achievement with someone supportive.

For larger milestones, mark progress with deliberate recognition. Options may include writing a letter to your future self that reflects the confidence or resilience you have built, creating a small visual reminder that represents a meaningful change, or sharing progress with an accountability partner, mentor, or support group to invite reflection and encouragement.

Celebration plays a practical role in growth. It strengthens memory, reinforces learning, and shapes how your mind interprets change. Recognizing progress helps frame the process as supportive and achievable. Small acknowledgments reinforce commitment and encourage continued effort, making progress feel rewarding and sustainable rather than demanding.

Continuing Education and Self-Compassion Practices

Personal growth requires ongoing attention and engagement. Sustained change depends on curiosity, skill development, and a consistent return to self-compassion as a core practice.

Learning supports growth in many ways. You may choose to read books or articles focused on emotional well-being, boundaries, or anxiety management. Short online courses can strengthen skills in mindfulness, cognitive behavioral approaches, or communication. Podcasts and virtual workshops led by experienced professionals can also provide insight and perspective.

Continued learning reinforces the understanding that growth is a process. Challenges and setbacks signal areas for skill refinement and reflection, not reasons to disengage. Exposure to new ideas keeps motivation steady and encourages flexibility in how you approach change.

Self-compassion remains essential throughout this process. High-functioning anxiety often connects with perfectionism and persistent self-criticism. Intentional self-kindness helps weaken those patterns and supports emotional balance. Simple practices can reinforce this mindset, including:

- Using a morning affirmation that acknowledges effort and progress

- Maintaining a calm, neutral inner dialogue when plans do not unfold as expected
- Allowing rest during periods of overwhelm without attaching guilt

Treating yourself with understanding supports resilience and consistency. Self-compassion strengthens your ability to continue learning, adapting, and progressing in a sustainable way. It provides the stability needed to maintain growth over the long term.

Troubleshooting Plateauing Motivation

Long-term efforts often reach plateaus, with slower progress, reduced motivation, or routines feeling stale. Early recognition and targeted strategies can help restore momentum without self-criticism.

Begin by assessing changes in your situation. Consider whether boredom with routines, competing commitments, or new stressors affect your motivation. Pinpointing the cause clarifies your response.

To address motivational plateaus, apply these strategies:

- ***Adjust your routines***. Change your self-care habits, introduce a new mindfulness practice, or set a short-term goal that sparks interest.
- ***Reconnect with your initial motivation***. Reflect on the reasons you began this process. Reviewing past journal

entries or the first chapter of this guide can renew your sense of purpose.

- ***Divide large goals into smaller, manageable steps***. Completing micro-tasks provides a sense of progress and accomplishment.
- ***Engage your support network***. Discuss challenges with an accountability partner, mentor, or peer group. External feedback and encouragement can boost energy and motivation.
- ***Practice self-compassion***. If symptoms of burnout appear, allow yourself time to rest. Resume your efforts when you feel ready, without judgment.

Plateaus represent natural pauses in personal growth. Treating these periods as opportunities for reassessment promotes patience and perspective. With the right approach, you can overcome motivational plateaus and continue your progress.

Planning for Future Growth and Balance

To maintain your progress, integrate planning and balance into your life well beyond the initial 30 days. This approach ensures ongoing development, even as daily demands change.

Schedule monthly or quarterly reviews as you would any important meeting. Use this time to evaluate:

- Your current stress and anxiety levels
- Boundaries that are working or need adjustment

- Routines that remain effective and those requiring improvement

Set new, achievable goals that reflect your changing needs. Focus on making meaningful changes, such as starting creative hobbies, establishing technology-free evenings, or expanding your support system.

Regularly assess your work-life balance. Honestly evaluate your energy, rest, and the proportion of obligations to restorative activities. Maintain this balance by making proactive adjustments before feeling overwhelmed.

Revisit foundational tools from earlier in this guide when needed. Skills like journaling, mindfulness, assertive communication, and boundary setting offer ongoing value.

At the end of each planning session, identify a specific action for the upcoming week or month and recognize your achievements. This approach grounds your progress in the present and prepares you for continued growth.

Measuring progress involves more than checking off tasks. It means taking ownership of your journey, learning from challenges and successes, and weaving growth into your daily routine. By using reflective practices, acknowledging achievements, investing in your development, responding thoughtfully to challenges, and planning for change, you transform short-term gains into lasting improvement.

As you transition from structured guidance, remember that growth is ongoing, unpredictable, and unique to each person. Continue to measure your progress by the consistency with which you support yourself with resilience and poise, as well as by your sense of calm and clarity. These habits form the foundation for enduring calm, clarity, and fulfillment.

Conclusion

As you reach the end of this guide, you have completed a focused 30-day process designed to build calm, clarity, and steadiness as a high-achieving woman. Throughout the previous chapters, you examined the roots of high-functioning anxiety, practiced techniques that support mental stillness, and applied tools that reinforce clear boundaries and sustainable routines. Each stage served as a practical step toward deeper self-connection and grounded leadership.

You now hold a set of skills that support daily balance. These include calming exercises, boundary-setting language, review practices that reduce mental clutter, and routines that promote consistency. You have also strengthened self-reflection, developed the ability to respond to setbacks without harsh judgment, and identified sources of support aligned with your needs. The structure of the 30-day process remains available to revisit and adapt when new pressures emerge or reinforcement becomes necessary.

Ongoing practice relies on awareness and intention. Some days will feel steady and centered, while others may bring familiar patterns of tension or urgency. This variation reflects normal life demands and periods of transition. Progress continues through regular self-check-ins, respect for personal limits, and attention to habits that protect well-being.

Thoughtful reflection helps you notice subtle shifts and respond with clarity before old patterns regain strength.

Continued growth benefits from curiosity and refinement. Writing, peer connection, and structured reflection practices help keep routines purposeful and flexible. With repetition, these skills integrate naturally into daily choices and leadership style.

This work strengthens mindful presence. Pausing, recalibrating, and leading with clarity models resilience and self-respect. Calm sharpens focus and deepens impact without diminishing ambition.

Moving forward, trust your capacity to meet stress with self-awareness and steadiness. Each intentional choice reinforces the connection between well-being and achievement. Professional guidance remains a supportive option when challenges feel heavy. This path continues to unfold through practice, reflection, and confidence in your ability to sustain calm.

FAQs

What is high-functioning anxiety, and how does it differ from other types of anxiety?

High-functioning anxiety involves ongoing worry, restlessness, or overthinking that exists alongside outward productivity and competence. Unlike more visible forms of anxiety, it may not involve panic attacks or obvious avoidance. Many individuals appear calm, capable, and successful while managing constant internal tension. Instead of withdrawing, they often respond through overperformance, perfectionism, or excessive responsibility. Symptoms tend to fuel activity and achievement, which can delay recognition and support.

Is this guide suitable for women with demanding work or family responsibilities?

Yes. This guide was designed for busy, high-achieving women. The routines and exercises focus on short, practical practices such as grounding and brief mindfulness moments that fit into full schedules. The 30-day structure allows gradual habit building and flexible pacing. Each strategy supports calm while aligning with existing professional and personal responsibilities.

Can I repeat or revisit chapters to reinforce my progress?

Yes. Repetition strengthens learning, especially with mindset and boundary skills. Returning to earlier chapters can offer new insights as circumstances shift. Many readers revisit specific exercises during periods of stress or transition and integrate them into regular routines.

What if I miss a day in the 30-day plan?

Missing a day is common when balancing multiple demands. A skipped practice does not undo progress. Reflect on what interfered and adjust expectations if needed. Resume when possible and focus on consistency across time rather than daily completion.

How do I know if my boundaries are working effectively?

Effective boundaries often lead to reduced overwhelm, less resentment, and greater ease when saying no. You may notice improved energy, fewer stress-related symptoms, and stronger self-respect. Regular reflection after challenging interactions can help assess whether adjustments are needed.

Do I need professional help, or is this guide enough?

This guide provides practical, evidence-informed strategies, but it does not replace individualized professional care in every situation. Therapy or counseling can offer tailored support, deeper exploration, and accountability. Professional help is recommended if anxiety significantly affects health, relationships, or daily functioning.

How can I motivate myself to sustain these practices after 30 days?

Sustained motivation comes from clear intentions, simple structure, and recognition of progress. Connect practices to daily routines, share goals with supportive people, and acknowledge small wins. Regular self-check-ins support adjustment and continuity.

References and Helpful Links

Leonard, E., PhD. (2023, July 25). Sense-of-self issues, weird worries, and more. Psychology Today.

Yaribeygi, H., Panahi, Y., Sahraei, H., Johnston, T. P., & Sahebkar, A. (2017). The impact of stress on body function: a review. PubMed, 16, 1057–1072.

Fakhri, Y., Jafarzadeh, S., Moradi, B., Zandsalimi, Y., Langarizadeh, G., Amirhajeloo, L., & Mirzaei, M. (2015). The non-carcinogenic risk of cadmium in bottled water in different age groups humans: Bandar Abbas City, Iran. Materia Socio Medica, 27(1), 52.

Keng, S., Smoski, M. J., & Robins, C. J. (2011). Effects of mindfulness on psychological health: A review of empirical studies. Clinical Psychology Review, 31(6), 1041–1056.

Kanter, J. W., Busch, A. M., Weeks, C. E., & Landes, S. J. (2008). The nature of clinical depression: Symptoms, syndromes, and behavior analysis. The Behavior Analyst, 31(1), 1–21.

Harvard Health. (2017, June 5). Q&A: The impact of stress.

Rainsberry, P. (2014, April 1). Donald Ingram Rice: 1965–1985: Constructing Certification in family medicine.

www.ingramcontent.com/pod-product-compliance
Lightning Source LLC
LaVergne TN
LVHW022015200926
848481LV00007B/2405
* 9 7 9 8 3 4 8 5 1 3 7 1 9 *